Mrs. Johnson's Rummage Sale
And Other Stewardship Dramas

Jeff Wedge

CSS Publishing Company, Inc., Lima, OH

MRS. JOHNSON'S RUMMAGE SALE

Copyright © 2003 by
CSS Publishing Company, Inc.
Lima, Ohio

The original purchaser may photocopy material in this publication for use as it was intended (i.e., worship material for worship use; educational material for classroom use; dramatic material for staging or production). No additional permission is required from the publisher for such copying by the original purchaser only. Inquiries should be addressed to: Permissions, CSS Publishing Company, Inc., P.O. Box 4503, Lima, Ohio 45802-4503.

For more information about CSS Publishing Company resources, visit our website at www.csspub.com or e-mail us at custserv@csspub.com or call (800) 241-4056.

ISBN 0-7880-1971-6   PRINTED IN U.S.A.

*To my mother
and my mother-in-law
who both finished
their stewardship of this life
last year.*

Table Of Contents

Introduction	7
Stewardship — *a drama about words*	11
What's A Tith-thee? — *a drama about understandings*	17
I Got Mail — *a drama about involvement*	21
Mrs. Johnson's Rummage Sale — *a drama about support*	27
Putting In Time — *a drama about participating*	33
Where'd It Come From? — *a drama about sources*	37
Build What? — *a drama about the stewardship of creation*	41

Introduction

One of the themes which comes up during the year in a church is stewardship. Many people hear the word *stewardship* as a synonym for *money*. For some people who share this understanding, a simple mention of the word — stewardship — is a signal to stop listening until the pitch for money is completed. One way to begin to resolve this problem is by presenting a drama which involves people before they realize the action has anything to do with stewardship. This is an indication that the word "stewardship" should likely be avoided in announcing the drama, as the first drama points out.

These dramas are about some aspects of stewardship. A complete study of the subject is really quite complex and demanding, and often far beyond the interest level of most parishioners. Thus, a stewardship program is used in many parishes to bring up the most important points for consideration. If these dramas are taken as a complete stewardship program, they are woefully incomplete. They do, however, offer a different way to introduce some stewardship concepts in a congregation, a way which might be easier for some people to hear. These dramas are meant to be used as part of a larger stewardship program.

Somebody might ask, "Why dramas?"

If you are reading this, you probably have a list of reasons of your own to answer that question. I would share at least one of my own. Dramas allow for different voices to present the Word in different ways than we are used to. Hearing the Word is not always easy, and many people suffer through more traditional methods of proclamation. Not, to be sure, that drama is particularly new. But in many places it has not been used recently, so it seems wonderfully fresh and attention-provoking.

Having this book in hand, there are some details that should be apparent as you look through the texts of the dramas. In general, you will find only minimal stage directions. This is intentional, in the interest of allowing the participants greater freedom of expression. Quite often an inexperienced player attempting to portray an emotion called for by the writer provides an unintentional source of humor, not a deeper insight into the character being portrayed. Thus, the idea here is to encourage the participants to be more natural.

In all of these scripts, props have been kept to the minimum. In general, anything needed should be readily available in the church building. Any other materials will normally be available at little additional cost. An hour is usually enough time to prepare the place where the dramas take place.

Names can present problems. Many of the names used here are intentionally ambiguous (they can be applied to either male or female players). If it happens that a role with a male name must be filled with a female player, the name should, of course, be changed accordingly. This does not mean the names should always be changed to the names of the players filling the roles. For many people using another name allows the freedom to act in ways an individual never would, at least in one's own persona.

Many of these dramas are intended to be a part of a worship service. In general they can be performed in a few minutes. These dramas do not present complete, rounded presentations of a particular point. Instead, they are generally meant to be provocative, which means they can easily be used as an introduction to a more complete explanation or as discussion starters. Of course, they can also be used in a variety of other ways, perhaps during a congregational meeting, as part of a dinner, perhaps as an entertainment during some other gathering, or even as the subject of a discussion. Have members of the group read the various parts, then discuss the action — either after the entire drama is read, or at critical points during the reading.

In many parishes the Youth Group is a ready source of players for dramas, and a number of these dramas involve youthful players. Using age specific players is not always required, depending on the skill levels available, but there are times when simply using available people may lead to unexpected consequences.

Some people think drama is simple to present, with little need for preparation or rehearsal. Perhaps it is as a result of personal experience in dramas that people think there is no big problem in presenting such things. It is this sort of thinking (and assuming) which most often leads to lousy dramas.

I once worked with a young lady who had a long list of dramatic credits. Even though she was only in high school, she had over a decade of experience on stage and television. She wanted to try directing, so she was offered the opportunity to direct a drama for a worship service. She recruited three other members of the Youth Group and they presented the drama. It did not go well.

The biggest problem was the tendency of those involved to clump together in a group, look at each other, and speak only as loudly as necessary for the rest of the group to hear. These are all very natural behaviors that must be carefully eliminated as a part of the rehearsal process. Of course, these behaviors tended to eliminate the rest of the congregation from the action, even if they did manage to hear what was going on (and most of them didn't).

Most of the problems weren't entirely the young lady's fault. She certainly would have benefitted from more guidance and coaching in the skills required of a director, but both of us assumed she knew all that stuff because of her experience.

She didn't, and it is possible that you also might gain from a quick review of some ways to help the people involved work with these dramas. Leaving aside all the questions of staging, blocking, use of props, and so on, this is a quick review of a few basic ways to help the people involved give better performances. There are four questions which make this easier.

Why is this person acting this way? The character has some particular things to say and some particular things to do in this drama. Why in the world would anybody say and do these things? The answer to this question calls for a certain amount of imagination and creativity, but it is crucial to the process of learning what is going on in a drama.

What did you say? James Garner has said, in interviews, that one of the experiences which helped him become a better actor was his early role on Broadway as a judge in *The Caine Mutiny*

Court Martial. He sat for the entire play without a single line. It quickly became apparent that this was a recipe for drowsiness. The cure was to listen intently to what each person said, as if he had never heard the words spoken before (even though he had spent months sitting and listening to exactly the same words night after night). Listening to what the others are saying and watching what they are doing is the best way to help everybody, yourself, the other players, and the people watching the drama unfold to focus on the action.

How would I say this if I was really in this situation? If this was actually happening, and you were really involved, some things would be more natural for you to say than others. The demands of a drama mean that some of the comments these characters make are rather artificial in the interest of moving the action along more quickly. But the point of this question is still one of developing your insight into the character you are playing. These are the words your character has to say. If this was real, how would you say this? Would you scream it, whisper it, speak blandly, angrily, with emphasis, intently, rapidly, slowly, or in some other way? Remember, even if there is no indication of how a line should be said, it is still important to say it naturally.

What gestures would I normally use? Some people are able to talk without moving any muscles below their shoulders. Other people seem unable to communicate without using most of their bodies to give emphasis to what they are saying. Too much of either extreme is, of course, too much. But some gestures are quite useful in making a point and emphasizing what is happening. Very few gestures are indicated in these scripts, and appropriate ones should be incorporated. But, beware of adding unnatural gestures. They often draw attention to the gesture (not the point) and away from the drama itself (which is the point).

Finally, and perhaps most importantly, when using these dramas, relax and have fun with them. There is often a humorous note involved, and it is not, contrary to the practice and apparent belief of some Christians, a sin to laugh. Please accept the invitation to relax and enjoy.

Stewardship

a drama about words

The Players
    Sam — a member who is conveniently hard of hearing
    Warren — a member of the stewardship committee
    Paula — a member who is hard of hearing at convenient times

The Setting
    Some members are walking around the church on a clean-up day. Wearing old clothes and carrying cleaning supplies should be all the sets and props needed. As the players are working, conversations begin.

(Sam and Warren enter from different directions. Both are carrying cleaning supplies and using them as they move toward each other)

Sam: Hey, Warren. How's it going?

Warren: Pretty good. How about you?

Sam: Oh, brother. I know the church needs to be cleaned thoroughly, but it sure is a tedious job. I wish we could afford to have a real cleaning crew come in and do this.

Warren: This can get to be boring, but it only happens once or twice a year. Besides, getting somebody to come in would probably be pretty expensive, especially when we can do the work ourselves.

Sam: Maybe, but it sure is a pain to do it.

Warren: But hiring somebody wouldn't be very good stewardship.

(*At the word "stewardship" Sam turns abruptly away from Warren and resumes cleaning*)

Warren: Sam?

Sam: Oh, hi Warren. How's it going?

Warren: Fine, fine ... Is something wrong?

Sam: Wrong? No, not really. Cleaning isn't my favorite occupation, but I guess we're making some progress.

Warren: Well, just a minute ago we were talking and you were suggesting we should hire somebody to clean up.

Sam: Well, I think that would be a good idea, if it wasn't too expensive.

Warren: Then I mentioned that hiring somebody to do something we could do wouldn't be good stewardship, and you ...

(*Sam again reacts to the word and resumes cleaning*)

Warren: Sam.

Sam: Oh, hi, Warren. How's it going?

Warren: I'm confused.

Sam: About what?

Warren: I think about you.

(*Paula enters, cleaning, and works her way toward Sam and Warren*)

Sam: Me? I'm just an ordinary guy. What's confusing about me?

Warren: Well, I don't mean to offend you, but twice now you have turned away in the middle of a conversation.

Sam: No. I don't remember doing anything like that ... But if I did, I am sorry. I really didn't mean to be rude.

Warren: Oh, that's all right. I just wish I knew what it was that started the whole episode.

(*Paula has cleaned her way into earshot*)

Paula: What whole episode? A new TV series?

Sam: No, not TV. Just something Warren thinks happened, but I'm not convinced it ever really did.

Warren: Well, twice Sam and I were talking about cleaning, and the possibility of hiring somebody to do it so we wouldn't have to.

Paula: I don't know. I like cleaning up once in a while. Gives me a feeling of accomplishment when I can see what I've done.

Warren: Yeah ... but then I pointed out that hiring somebody from outside probably wouldn't be good stewardship ...

(*Sam reacts to the word once again, but Warren and Paula don't notice*)

Warren: ... and Sam just started ignoring me.

Paula: Well, that sounds a little rude. You don't think there's a chance we might hire somebody from outside, do you? I really like these clean-up days. They give me a feeling that I've really done something for the church.

Warren: No, I don't think clean-up days will ever be something we hire out. If we can do it ourselves, why have somebody from the outside do it and send us their bill?

Paula: Oh, good. I'm glad these won't be changing.

Warren: (*Looks around*) Where'd Sam go?

Paula: (*Looks around as well*) Oh, he's over there.

Warren: See, he did it again.

Paula: What?

Warren: He walked away in the middle of a conversation again.

Paula: No, he didn't do that.

Warren: You were standing right here. You saw him!

Paula: No, Sam just heard the word "stewardship." He always stops listening when he hears that word.

Warren: Are you kidding me?

Paula: No. Watch ... Sam!

Sam: Oh, hi, Paula. What's happening?

Paula: Nothing much. You getting lots of cleaning done?

Sam: Oh, yeah. It's going pretty well.

Warren: Stewardship.

(*Sam again reacts to the word*)

Warren: Well, I'll be. I wonder how that happened?

Paula: Oh, it's just the result of too many stewardship sermons over the years.

Warren: I've never seen anything like it.

Paula: Oh, Sam just has an advanced case. But lots of people are like that.

Warren: They hear the word and they stop listening?

Paula: That's about it.

Warren: But it doesn't affect you?

Paula: Oh, no. I know a simple little word won't hurt me.

Warren: Stewardship.

Paula: See? Nothing. No effect.

Warren: Well, I'm on the Stewardship Committee this year and I was wondering ...

(*Paula reacts to the term "stewardship committee" and begins cleaning furiously*)

Warren: I can tell, this is going to be a very lonely year.

(*All exit*)

What's A Tith-thee?

a drama about understandings

The Players
    Fred — a member with a problem understanding a word he's seen a lot recently
    Chris — chair of the finance committee

The Setting
    A table has all the items needed for a coffee table after the worship service — a coffee pot, cups, creamer, sugar, spoons, and so forth. A plate of cookies or doughnuts can also be placed on the table.

Note: This drama is based on a question once actually asked of a pastor by a pronunciationally-challenged parishioner. Everything beyond the question and mispronunciation which form the basis for the drama is drawn from the writer's imagination.
    Pronounce the word in question with at least *two* syllables: "TITH ... thee." The pronunciation should rhyme with "pithy."

~~~~

(*Fred enters and pours himself a cup of coffee. Chris enters after Fred and walks over to the table*)

Chris: Did you make the coffee?

Fred: No, I think Mrs. Johnson made it.

Chris: Oh, good. Then I can have some safely.

Fred: Well, I think I make a pretty good cup of coffee. When I was in the Army, I made coffee strong enough to put hair on your chest!

Chris: I'm not sure that's a recommendation.

Fred: We did have a rule, though. The first one to complain had to make the next pot of coffee.

Chris: (*Thinks for a minute*) I'm sure you make a fine pot of coffee, Fred. (*Pours a cup*)

Fred: Thanks. (*Stirs his coffee as he watches Chris*) Are you still chair of the Finance Committee?

Chris: Let me warn you, if I hear any complaints, you might be nominated as the next chair of the Finance Committee.

Fred: Oh, no complaints. I just have a question for you. (*Looks around before asking his question, doesn't speak*)

Chris: (*Looks around with Fred*) Did you want to ask a question?

Fred: Well, yes. But I'm a little embarrassed about it.

(*Both look around again*)

Chris: Go ahead; ask anything. If I can, I'll give you an answer. If I can't, we'll go find out.

Fred: Okay. (*A last glance around*) What's a tith-thee?

Chris: A what?

Fred: A tith-thee.

Chris: I don't think I've ever heard of a ... what'd you call it, again?

Fred: A tith-thee.

Chris: A tith-thee? ... No, I've never heard of that. Where'd you hear about it?

Fred: You must've heard of it. Don't you even read the stuff your committee sends out? It's all over it.

Chris: Tith-thee?

Fred: That's right.

Chris: Well, what do we say about it?

Fred: Stuff like everybody should consider a tith-thee — and how everybody should really be tith-thee-ing, or at least working toward that goal of being a tith-thee-er. Stuff like that.

Chris: Huh?

Fred: Well, it's a fine thing, when you don't even know what your own committee is telling people to do.

Chris: I honestly have never heard of a tith-thee, as least as far as I know.

Fred: Then I guess I don't have to worry much about all that stuff your committee is sending out about a tith-thee. (*Begins to walk away*)

Chris: (*Begins to have an idea of what is going on*) Fred, wait a minute.

Fred: What?

Chris: How do you spell it?

Fred: What?

Chris: A tith-thee.

Fred: T - I - T - H - E. Tith-thee!

Chris: (*Tries very hard not to laugh out loud*) Oh, you mean a tithe!

Fred: Do I?

Chris: I think so.

Fred: So I just can't pronounce the word, huh?

Chris: It sounds like it.

Fred: Well, then I guess your committee isn't trying to put some new gimmick in place. Tithing's been around for a long time.

Chris: It certainly has.

Fred: So, I guess I'm safe. Nobody is going to nominate me to be chair of the Finance Committee. I'm not going to complain about something like tithing.

Chris: I guess I won't find a replacement today.

(*Both exit*)

I Got Mail

a drama about involvement

The Players
    Paul — a young member of the Youth Group
    Joan — another young member of the Youth Group
    Billie — the oldest member of the Youth Group
    Chris — an older kid, but only newly a member of the Youth Group
    Pat — a member of the Youth Group who has become Chris' friend

The Situation
The Youth Group meeting is just breaking up and the members are leaving the room where the meeting has taken place. The action takes place just outside the door to the meeting room. A simple sign reading "Youth Room" is really all the set requires, more elaborate settings are certainly possible, if desired.

(*Paul and Joan enter*)

Paul: (*Pulls an envelope from his pocket*) Hey, Joan. Did you get one of these in the mail yesterday?

Joan: No. What is it?

Paul: A letter from the church, and something called a "Time and Talent" sheet. They want to know what I want to do around the church next year.

Joan: Let me see. (*Reaches for the envelope, opens it, and unfolds the papers inside*)

(*Billie enters*)

Paul: (*Points at papers in Joan's hand*) Hey, Billie. Did you get one of these in the mail yesterday?

Billie: (*Looks at papers over Joan's shoulder*) Yeah. You get one every year.

Paul: No kidding? I never got one before.

Joan: (*Hands the papers back to Paul*) I still haven't gotten one, unless it's in the mail today.

Billie: Don't worry, you'll get one soon enough. Sometimes it takes a couple of days for the mail to get out. But soon enough you'll get one of these in the mail, too.

Paul: How come I never got one before this?

Billie: That's right, you only affirmed your faith this year, didn't you?

Paul: Yeah. So what?

Billie: In this church these things mostly get sent to adult members. That's probably why you haven't gotten any until now.

Paul: But, am I reading this right? They'll let me do the stuff on this sheet now?

Billie: Remember what pastor said in class? It's not they; it's us. And now you're more a part of the us than ever before. So, to phrase it the right way, we're always looking for people who want to do stuff around here. Sign up for something, and you'll probably be doing it before too long.

Paul: Hey, cool. I can be an usher, or a money counter!

Joan: And I can work in the nursery.

Billie: Sure. You can do all that sort of stuff.

(*Chris and Pat enter*)

Paul: I better fill this out right away and turn it in before I leave. That way I won't lose the sheet.

Chris: Turn what in? Are we supposed to turn something in for the Youth Group?

Billie: No. Nothing like that. Paul got his Time and Talent sheet in the mail, and he wants to get busy right away doing stuff around the church.

Chris: Oh, those things. They don't mean anything.

Paul: What?

Chris: They don't mean anything. Nobody reads them. All they really care about is the card that says how much money you're going to give.

Joan: What card? What money?

(*Everyone ignores Joan*)

Paul: The Time and Talent sheet really doesn't mean anything?

Chris: Yeah, it really doesn't.

Billie: That's not the way it's worked out for me.

Chris: Well, maybe not for you, but that's the way it's worked out for me. My family moved here last summer, but the church we used to belong to always used Time and Talent sheets, too.

Billie: Lots of churches use them.

Chris: Yeah. Lots of churches pass them out and never look at them again. I volunteered to be an usher for three years straight in my other church, and I never even got a call to tell me I couldn't do it. Those sheets are a joke.

Billie: That was a different church. Fill the sheet out in this church, say you want to be an usher, and you'll probably be on the next schedule to come out.

Chris: Is this church that different from my old church? I doubt it. All churches are the same. The only response I ever got from my Time and Talent sheet was when they called and asked why I wasn't up to date on my pledge. All they wanted was my money.

Pat: It sounds like all they wanted was money, sure enough.

Billie: Well, sometimes churches have trouble with this stewardship thing. It can be difficult to make use of everyone who volunteers for something around the church.

Chris: And that's why all anybody in the church really cares about is how much money you give, not what you want to do.

Paul: Then why even bother to send out Time and Talent sheets? It looks to me like it must cost something for the paper and copying and everything. Wouldn't it be cheaper just to send out the pledge cards? (*Holds up Time and Talent sheet as he speaks*)

Joan: That makes sense.

Chris: I never really thought about that. I guess I always figured there was a rule that there had to be a Time and Talent sheet, or something.

Billie: Actually, if Time and Talent sheets aren't going to be used, the work of copying them and distributing them and the cost would all be examples of rather poor stewardship, wouldn't they?

Chris: Yeah, I guess so. Certainly would be a waste of money, anyway.

Pat: So if we don't let people do the stuff they volunteer for, are we being poor stewards?

(*All exit*)

Mrs. Johnson's Rummage Sale

a drama about support

The Players

    Mrs. Eleanor Johnson — a pillar of her community and her church, the main force behind the rummage sale

    Pastor Smith — pastor of the church, quiet but not weak when it matters

    Helen Cuthbert — Mrs. Johnson's faithful friend

    Howard Gordon — a Youth Group member

The Situation

    It looks like a normal day around the church. The newsletter went out late last week and there aren't any big jobs to be done today. The action which is about to begin takes place in the hall outside the church office, but can be staged almost anywhere. A sign should suffice to indicate the location of the office.

Mrs. Johnson: (*A well-dressed woman enters explosively, carrying a newsletter which she waves around, obviously very upset about something. Mutters as she searches angrily*) Where is that little skunk! ... Where? ... Oh-h-h-h-h ... Where is that *person*? ... I'll find 'em, and when I do, it won't be pretty ... (*Comments continue as long as needed while she looks for someone in various places. Finally, she shouts*) Where is that pastor?

Pastor Smith: (*Enters calmly, speaks reasonably*) Hello, Mrs. Johnson. Are you looking for me?

Mrs. Johnson: (*Loudly*) You bet I am. (*Waves newsletter at Pastor Smith*) What's the meaning of this?

Pastor Smith: (*Intentionally misunderstanding her*) That's the newsletter. We send it out to keep the members of the congregation informed about the things that are happening here.

Mrs. Johnson: Oh, really?

Pastor Smith: Really. You should be pleased. There's a whole page devoted to your rummage sale in that issue.

Mrs. Johnson: And you can actually stand there and say that? After the way you wrote the announcement? You can say I should be pleased?

Pastor Smith: Actually I didn't write the announcement, but it seemed like you would appreciate the amount of space devoted to it.

Mrs. Johnson: (*Very loudly this time*) Just look at *what* it says! Read the stupid thing! (*Thrusts the newsletter at Pastor Smith*)

Pastor Smith: (*Opens the newsletter, turns the pages*) Let's see, here ... Ah, yes ... Here it is. (*Turns to the announcement*) Here's a real nice graphic, and then the text. It says, "Announcing Mrs. Johnson's Rummage Sale. Bring all your rummage to ..."

Mrs. Johnson: Wait! Don't you understand? That announcement makes it sound like the rummage sale is for me, not the church.

Pastor Smith: (*Looks at the announcement*) Oh, I don't think so. It says right here, "Proceeds to benefit the library fund."

Mrs. Johnson: That's at the bottom of the page, and in small type. The top of the page says, "MRS. JOHNSON'S RUMMAGE SALE." It sounds like the rummage sale is for me.

Pastor Smith: Well, maybe. But I don't think anyone will interpret it that way ... Do you? (*Returns the newsletter*)

Mrs. Johnson: I don't have to think. I know people will interpret it that way. In fact, I've already gotten three phone calls from people trying to find out how bad it is, since we have to have a rummage sale at church to help bail us out of the financial situation we're in. My husband is furious, because he's gotten four calls at his office asking the same thing.

Pastor Smith: Oh. Well, I'm really sorry about the misunderstanding, but you know you *were* the leader in the effort to hold a rummage sale. In fact, I'm sure there wouldn't have been any rummage sale if you hadn't pushed quite as hard as you did. In some ways, many folks around here have started to think of it as Mrs. Johnson's rummage sale.

Mrs. Johnson: (*Folds her arms, looks disgusted*) I hate that name.

Helen Cuthbert: (*Enters behind Pastor Smith*) Oh, Ellie. I thought I heard your voice. Have you seen the newsletter? Isn't it just wonderful that the sale has a whole page of publicity?

Mrs. Johnson: No, it isn't wonderful. It's terrible.

Helen Cuthbert: Terrible? ... No ... It's wonderful. They printed everything I gave them about the rummage sale.

Mrs. Johnson: You gave them?

Helen Cuthbert: Sure. You asked me to do publicity for the sale, so I wrote up the announcement for the newsletter and turned it in two Sundays ago.

Mrs. Johnson: And you called it "Mrs. Johnson's Rummage Sale"?

Helen Cuthbert: Well, certainly. You should get the credit, after all you've done to get permission for the sale, even when so many people were opposed.

Pastor Smith: (*Clears throat noisily*) Ah ...

Helen Cuthbert: Oh, that's right. You didn't want to have a rummage sale, did you, Pastor?

Pastor Smith: I was one of the people who opposed the idea.

(*Howard Gordon enters carrying a box full of what can only be described as junk*)

Helen Cuthbert: I never did understand that, completely. It seems like such a good idea, and the church can certainly use the money a rummage sale will raise.

Pastor Smith: There are a great many reasons why this sale could be thought of as less than a good idea. For example ...

Howard Gordon: (*Interrupts*) Hey, Mrs. Johnson?

Mrs. Johnson: Yes, Howard?

Howard Gordon: My mother told me to bring this stuff over to church for your rummage sale. I guess if there's anything you can use, though, you can just take it. (*Sets the box down with a clatter*)

Mrs. Johnson: (*Grimaces at the noise of the box*) Thank you, Howard. But I really don't think there's anything I can use.

Howard Gordon: Really? Well, I guess you can just throw any of this junk out if you can't sell it. We cleaned it out of the garage.

Mrs. Johnson: Thank you for your concern, Howard.

(*Howard exits*)

Helen Cuthbert: Wasn't that nice of the Gordons? To send over all this stuff for your rummage sale, Ellie?

Mrs. Johnson: (*Ignores Helen, picks up something from the box with two fingers*) What in the world could this possibly be? (*Drops it back in the box*)

(*All exit*)

Putting In Time

a drama about participating

The Players
    Harry — a member who doesn't always listen
    Sheila — a member who listens more attentively

The Situation
    People are leaving the sanctuary after the worship service.

(Harry and Sheila enter)

Harry: I don't believe it.

Sheila: What?

Harry: I just don't believe it.

Sheila: Now what's wrong?

Harry: *(Motions back toward the sanctuary)* Didn't you hear?

Sheila: Hear what?

Harry: All that stuff about my time.

Sheila: What stuff?

Harry: About how I'm supposed to give up my time, now.

Sheila: What, now?

Harry: Huh?

Sheila: Time has always been something we should give to the church.

Harry: Maybe ... but what's this sudden emphasis on my time?

Sheila: A sudden emphasis?

Harry: Yeah, all of a sudden, my time is a subject for discussion.

Sheila: The way we spend our time was mentioned in the sermon.

Harry: Yeah, see ... you heard it, too.

Sheila: But it isn't a sudden emphasis.

Harry: Well, I never heard anything about time until just recently. It seems to me like time is the new thing — the new emphasis — the new way to get more out of me.

Sheila: Seems to me time has always been a part of this.

Harry: Maybe, but not like this.

Sheila: Do you object to giving some of your time?

Harry: (*Pauses while he considers the question*) Well, yeah, sort of.

Sheila: What?

Harry: Hey, don't misunderstand me. I'm not some sort of cheapskate. I give a substantial contribution each week. I even make it up when I miss a Sunday. And I'm here most weeks. But why should

I be expected to give up my free time in addition to my weekly contribution?

Sheila: What?

Harry: I work hard at my job, and I work pretty long hours, and I try to spend most of my free time with the family.

Sheila: That sounds good.

Harry: Well, at least I did, until now, when all of a sudden the church wants my free time, too.

Sheila: Does it have to be a choice?

Harry: Maybe I could bring the kids to the clean-up crew on Saturday morning. I'm sure the boys would enjoy driving the lawn mower. And it might be good practice for their driving tests in a few years.

Sheila: That might be less than helpful.

Harry: See, I'd probably end up spending all my time trying to keep them out of the way of all the other folks who are actually doing some work. I doubt I'd be much help.

Sheila: Maybe you could help out by being in the nursery. That way other parents could come help out.

Harry: Me? In the nursery? I don't think so!

Sheila: It was just a thought.

Harry: Look, I always figured people who couldn't afford to provide much financial support gave lots of time to the church.

Sheila: Sort of a trade-off?

Harry: Exactly.

Sheila: But you ...

Harry: I give a substantial amount each week. It just isn't fair that all of a sudden I'm supposed to give *both* my time *and* money.

(*Both freeze, then exit*)

Where'd It Come From?

a drama about sources

The Players
   Sharon — A nursery helper who has just finished a session in the nursery
   Philip — A friend of Sharon

The Setting
   Sharon and Philip meet somewhere around the church.

~~~~~~

(*Sharon enters, looks intently at things. Philip enters, watches Sharon*)

Philip: What are you doing?

Sharon: Oh, hi, Philip.

Philip: Hi. What are you doing?

Sharon: (*Resumes staring at things*) Looking.

Philip: Looking?

Sharon: Yes, looking.

Philip: Let me try this again. What are you doing?

Sharon: (*Laughs a little*) I'm sorry. I was just playing a game with the little kids in the nursery. I guess I'm still playing all by myself.

Philip: What game?

Sharon: Where'd it come from?

Philip: Where'd what come from?

Sharon: No, that's the name of the game — Where'd it come from?

Philip: I've never heard of it.

Sharon: Really? Well, it's a very simple game, and you don't even need any equipment to play.

Philip: Okay, now I'm curious. How does it work?

Sharon: One of the kids really got it started. She was so proud of her new dress because her aunt made it for her.

Philip: Huh?

Sharon: Well, that's the way it works. You start with something, anything really, and you go back to where it came from.

Philip: So the dress came from the aunt. I guess this *is* a game for the little kids.

Sharon: Well, the aunt is only the first step.

Philip: First step?

Sharon: Sure. After all, the aunt got the cloth somewhere.

Philip: I think I'm getting the picture. The aunt buys the cloth at the fabric store, makes the dress, and gives it to her niece.

Sharon: So, where'd it come from?

Philip: What, the fabric store?

Sharon: That would be an interesting question, but let's keep it simple. The fabric, where'd it come from?

Philip: I suppose it came from somebody who made it, probably the mill.

Sharon: So where'd that come from?

Philip: Not the mill, you mean the raw material they used to make the fabric?

Sharon: That's right.

Philip: I imagine, if the dress was cotton ...

Sharon: It was.

Philip: ... then the cotton must have come from a farmer who grows cotton.

Sharon: And the farmer ...

Philip: We all know where the farmer came from.

Sharon: Not the farmer, the cotton.

Philip: Well, the farmer probably bought the seed from somebody.

Sharon: And where'd the seed come from?

Philip: Somebody had to grow the plants that produced the seed.

Sharon: And then what?

Philip: What do you mean?

Sharon: Then what? Where'd it come from?

Phillip: What?

Sharon: Is that where it ends? Or did the seeds start from somewhere, too?

(*Sharon and Philip freeze, then exit*)

Build What?

a drama about the stewardship of creation

The Players
- Matt — an avid camper
- Sam — another avid camper
- Mr. Daniels — the Youth Group advisor
- Lucy — a camper, but reasonable
- Meredith — not very excited by camping
- Hank — a fairly new member of the Youth Group

The Situation

People are starting to gather for the Youth Group meeting, which is supposed to start in a few minutes. A discussion begins before the meeting.

The set can be simply a few chairs scattered around the performance area. Other furnishings for the room where the Youth Group would meet can be added as desired, but only enough to set the mood, not enough to detract from the action.

(Matt and Sam enter and begin arranging chairs for the meeting)

Matt: Hey, did you hear what happened to our campground?

Sam: What?

Matt: Did you hear about the campground?

Sam: You mean old Mr. Hodgkins' place, where we go camping each spring?

Matt: Yeah, the place where we *used* to go camping each spring and sometimes in the fall. Remember old Mr. Hodgkins died last year?

Sam: Yeah. The funeral was in the church.

Matt: Well, in his will, the land went to his four kids. Now it turns out they couldn't decide how to split up the land, so they had to sell it.

Sam: So what? We'll still be able to camp there, won't we?

Matt: I doubt it. The guy who bought the land just announced his plans to build a shopping center on the land.

Sam: (*Disbelieving*) A shopping center? On our campground?

(*Mr. Daniels enters during the next speech. He is carrying some papers*)

Matt: Yeah, a shopping center. Maybe we can go camping at the sporting goods store, if they have one.

Sam: How do you know about this?

Matt: My dad heard it on the news, then he showed me an article in the paper.

Mr. Daniels: Talking about the place where we used to go camping?

Sam: Used to? You mean it's true?

Mr. Daniels: I'm afraid so.

Matt: The land's been sold, and they're going to build a shopping center. We'll never find another campsite as nice as that one.

(*Lucy and Meredith enter*)

Sam: This day is sure depressing all of a sudden.

Lucy: Thanks, Sam. I'm glad to see you, too.

Sam: Oh, I didn't mean you. I just found out about our campground. They're going to build a shopping center on it.

Meredith: Well, that might be nice. Some new stores to look in when I want to go shopping couldn't hurt.

Matt: But we won't be able to go camping there any more.

Meredith: Well, personally, I'd rather go shopping than camping anyway.

Lucy: That's because the only camping trip you ever went on was the one when it rained the whole time. Nobody had much fun that week.

Matt: Actually, I got to like eating cold baked beans that week. And the devotions around the fire, with everybody sitting on wet logs, and the rain kept putting out the fire. Remember that one, Mr. Daniels?

Mr. Daniels: I think we can move on and get the meeting started.

Lucy: Mr. Daniels, how long did it take for your eyebrows to grow back after the gasoline you used to light that fire finally caught?

Mr. Daniels: Too long, but not as long as you'll be reminding me about it, I guess.

Matt: And now we won't ever get to go camping again.

Mr. Daniels: Why not?

Matt: Because they're going to build a shopping center on our campground. Haven't you been paying attention?

Mr. Daniels: Why? Is that the only place we can go camping?

Lucy: It might not be the only, but it was the best.

Sam: I've got an idea. Why don't we stop 'em from building that shopping center?

Matt: Hey, good idea.

Sam: Yeah. Maybe we can explain, and they wouldn't build it.

Mr. Daniels: Maybe we could write a letter, or even ask for an appointment to explain the situation.

Matt: That won't do anything. A bunch of kids want to camp there a couple of times a year? They'll still build the shopping center.

Mr. Daniels: The shopping center might get built, but it certainly wouldn't hurt anything to let the people building it know about our concerns.

Lucy: I think what we need is something dramatic.

Meredith: Like what?

Lucy: Well, maybe we could find out who is planning to build the shopping center and TP his house.

Meredith: What?

Lucy: You know, go over to the house and wrap it in toilet paper some night. Or we could just wrap the bushes in front.

Meredith: Where do you people get these ideas?

Sam: I don't know, but this might be fun.

Mr. Daniels: It might be, but there might be a couple of problems with it, too.

Lucy: Like what?

Mr. Daniels: In the first place, it could certainly be considered illegal and that would get everybody in trouble.

Meredith: That's enough for me. Besides, I like the idea of another shopping center in town, remember?

Mr. Daniels: There is another problem. Exactly what would you be saying by wrapping a house in toilet paper?

Lucy: Huh? Saying?

Mr. Daniels: Saying. What message would you be giving to the person who will be developing the land?

Lucy: We'd be telling everybody what we think of the idea of building a shopping center. It should be flushed along with the paper.

Matt: I like that message.

Mr. Daniels: Perhaps, but what's the rule we always follow when we leave the campsite?

Sam: You mean about leaving it cleaner than we found it?

Mr. Daniels: That's the one. Perhaps your method isn't completely appropriate for the message you want to convey.

Matt: Maybe not, but we'd be saving a wonderful campsite from becoming another dress shop.

Meredith: What's wrong with another dress shop?

Matt: There are already more dress shops than campsites. Can't we keep the campsite?

Sam: It doesn't look like it.

Matt: Why not? Can't we keep them from tearing up the place?

Mr. Daniels: We can certainly investigate the possibilities, but we do need to be careful. After all, we do represent this church. We certainly want to do things the right way.

Lucy: You know, camping is fun, but we can always do something else.

Matt: Well, I want to go camping, and I want to go camping at our campsite.

Sam: Hey, why don't we chain ourselves to the trees?

Meredith: What?

Sam: I saw it on a TV show. They chained themselves to the trees to stop the developer from destroying a park. By the end of the show the park was saved. We could do that to save the campground.

Mr. Daniels: It's an interesting idea, but you could get hurt.

Meredith: Besides, when do we have to do this? I have a date next Friday to go to the dance, and I'm not missing it to be chained to some tree.

Sam: Well, it worked on TV. But maybe it wasn't such a good idea after all.

(*Hank enters very excitedly*)

Matt: There's nothing we can do, I guess.

Hank: Hey, did you hear?

Matt: Hear what?

Hank: They're going to build a new shopping center in town. And my dad just got hired to be construction superintendent.

Matt: What?

Hank: (*Slows down*) My dad works for a construction company. He bought a house here because we really liked the town, but so far it's meant he has to travel to the construction site each week. Now he'll be working right here. He'll be home most of the time for the next couple of years until the shopping center is finished. Isn't it great?

Matt: Great for you, maybe. Not for the rest of us.

Hank: I guess I can't expect anybody else to be as excited as I am, but this is great for me.

Matt: Oh, we're all happy for you. That's not the problem.

Sam: Yeah. The problem is the shopping center.

Lucy: The shopping center is being built on the land we used for our camping trips.

Meredith: Well, I think it's great Hank's father is going to be home for a while. I'm really happy for him. Besides, who liked that old camping stuff, anyway?

Matt, Sam, and Lucy: WE DID!

Hank: Actually, I like going camping, too. Have you ever gone on a river trip?

Matt: Yeah, we tried that once. But the best place is where your dad is going to build a shopping center. We've been going there for a lot of years, and it's almost like our home away from home.

Sam: Yeah. It's the coolest place to go camping.

Meredith: As long as it doesn't rain.

Lucy: The place is really lovely, a little stream and deep, thick pine needles, a wonderful place, just like a dream forest.

Mr. Daniels: It is a good camping site, but it doesn't look like we'll be able to use it very much longer.

Lucy: It doesn't look like we'll be able to use it at all.

Matt: Maybe we could start a petition drive to stop the shopping center. After all, the woods we camped in will probably be pretty much destroyed.

Sam: Yeah, maybe we could picket the developer's office. We could carry signs about the destruction of the environment.

Mr. Daniels: Those suggestions are, at least, much more reasonable than some of your earlier thoughts.

Hank: But what about my dad?

Matt: Well, it's not like he won't have a job somewhere.

Hank: No, but it is like he won't have a job *here*, where we can go to a ball game like you told me you did with your dad a couple of weeks ago.

Matt: (*Defensively*) You'd still be able to go on the weekends, when he comes home.

Sam: Yeah, there have to be some games on the weekend.

Mr. Daniels: But, it still means Hank's father wouldn't be home during the week.

Lucy: That must be hard.

Hank: It sure isn't easy, but that's the way it's been for a long time now. I guess that's why I was looking forward so much to having dad around.

Matt: What about our campsite?

(*All freeze, then all exit*)